THE BIG BOOK OF BUCKY VOL. 1

Luke had Yoda. The Karate Kid had Mr. Miyagi. Up until now, working out exactly what to do with a fresh set of Buckyballs was more or less a solitary pursuit. No more. Consider The Big Book of Bucky, Vol. 1 the Magna Carta of Magnets; the road map that turns your Buckys from a cube you're scared to touch into a magical pile of quicksilver that shape-shifts effortlessly in your hands. And, as is the Bucky way, we've packed it to the gills with fun facts, games, and more! Not bad, right?

THANK YOU.

It's hard to believe but...

In the beginning, Buckyballs was just two guys, hand-stuffing magnets into jars in New York City.

Before landing in the pages of Rolling Stone and People magazine, before Google's home page linked to the search for "Buckyball" (and nearly exploded our computers), and before 1 million individual Buckyballs sold in a single day, one guy cut labels, the other took the boxes to the post office. One guy designed the website, the other figured out how to make it run.

Neither of them were particularly skilled shape-makers though; they just liked mashing the balls around in their hands for fun. You knew what to do though! In spite of the fact that, at the start, Buckyballs came with absolutely no instructions, you started building. More importantly, you started sharing pictures of your builds with us and your fellow Ballers in places like Facebook and Flickr.

Slowly, the world began to take notice. Gizmodo, College Humor, Boing-Boing, Huffington Post, Swiss-Miss, and Geekology all championed this new desk-top trend. ThinkGeek brought it to the masses online. Brookstone and Urban Outfitters launched it in retail after we developed the now iconic floating-balls packaging.

Meanwhile, social networking was turning Buckyballs from a simple desktoy into a community of creative, desk-bound, fun-seekers, sharing pictures, tips, tricks, and more. This book is the collection of all of that wisdom, humor, and thousands of hours of Buckyballin'.

So where does it go from here? It's hard to say. In your hands is The Big Book of Bucky Vol. 1. But the next chapter, maybe even the whole next volume, starts with you.

How fun is that?

- Bucky

WHY BUCKYBALLS AREN'T FOR KIDS

Magnets are serious fun for adults, but they also pose a serious threat. If swallowed or ingested, they can connect across intestines causing blockages, perforations, or worse. The repercussions can be deadly. For this reason, the warning on the box reads "Keep Out Of Reach Of All Children!" It's important that you take it seriously.

DON'T
- Give Buckyballs to children.
- Put them near your mouth, nose, or lips.
- Play with them on or near anyone with a pacemaker or similar medical device.
- Store them in close proximity to credit cards, computers or other exposed or delicate magnetic storage devices.

DO
- Enjoy Buckyballs on desks and in dorm rooms.
- Experiment. Buckyballs are great for finding studs in walls, fishing keys out of hard to reach places, and who knows what else?
- Share 'em with a friend. You might not have much choice in the matter once they see them in your hands - ugh.

⚠**WARNING**

Keep Away From All Children!
Do not put in nose or mouth.
Swallowed magnets can stick to intestines causing serious injury or death.
Seek immediate medical attention if magnets are swallowed or inhaled.

BASIC **SHAPES**

The Infinite Monkey Theorem
states that given unlimited time, and a
keyboard to randomly pound on, even
a monkey will eventually produce the
complete works of William Shakespeare.
Unfortunately, trying to figure out the
cube on your own without so much as a
hint can leave you feeling dumber than a
chimp. Now for the good news: Everything
changes the second you turn the page.
Soon you'll be walking upright with pride.

The Fun Starts Here.

THE **TUBE**

Admit it, you crunched-up the cube before you even opened the book, right? It's cool. We're going to turn that messy pile in your hands into a tube. First though you're going to need lure a chain from the tangled mess. Grab a ball or two and pull gently. It takes a special touch, but you'll get it.

Wrap the chain around your finger and—boom—you've got a tube!

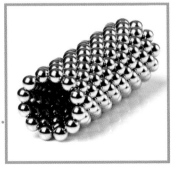

GET **IN LINE**

Lined Up. We're going to be taking a lot about balls here: This is what they look like lined up. Notice how every ball has a buddy? They come in pairs, just like, well, you know... balls.

Interlocked. In this formation, the balls in one line fill the grooves in the other. They're NOT perfectly lined up. It's cool though, interlocked can be useful at times too; the bond between the balls is stronger in this configuration.

PRO TIP

Balls not snapping together properly in your chain? Two shapes not attaching to one another the way you want them to, interlocking when you want them lined up and vice versa? Try flipping one side over. Magnets are funny, but flipping them fixes it 99% of the time.

BASIC SHAPES

THE **SHEET**

There's more than one way to skin a cat. Making sheets is kind of like that —there's two ways—only no felines are injured in the process. None.

Way #1: The Wrap
Simply wrap your chain around a single ball and keep going and going. What will emerge is a hexagonal sheet with interlocking balls that just keeps growing until you've run out of chain.

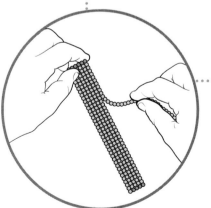

Way #2: The Zig-Zag
Again, starting with your balls in chain, zig and zag them back and forth, folding at the highlighted balls. The sheets you make this way should be lined up.

POP QUIZ

Can you spot how each of the sheets below was made? One was made by Zig-Zagging, the other by Wrapping. We've cropped the photo to make it harder, but don't over-think it; even a blind man has a 50% chance of getting it right.

A

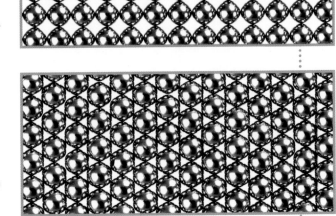
B

ANSWER: A was made by Zig-Zagging. You can tell cause the balls are lined up. B was made by wrapping. See the interlocking balls? Good.

THE 6x6 CUBE 〔216 Balls〕

Your Buckyballs looked this when you got 'em.
Time to put 'em back. We'll show you how.

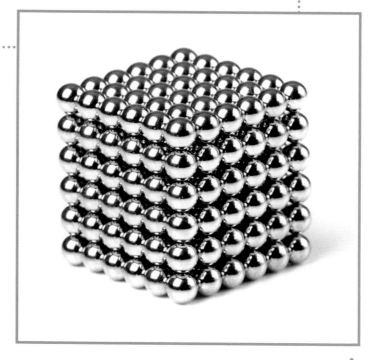

There are times when it's fun to figure things out on your own —life, love, foreign transit systems—this is not one of those times. If left to your own devices, you'd probably just keep trying to pound the thing flat like an angry bird. Truth is, making cubes is more about folding than forcing. You'll see.

1 Start by making a sheet 36 balls long and 6 balls wide by zigging and zagging your chain back and forth. It's going to take 216 balls in total.

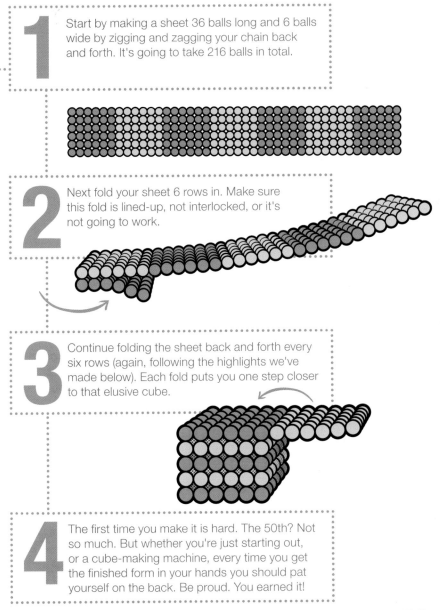

2 Next fold your sheet 6 rows in. Make sure this fold is lined-up, not interlocked, or it's not going to work.

3 Continue folding the sheet back and forth every six rows (again, following the highlights we've made below). Each fold puts you one step closer to that elusive cube.

4 The first time you make it is hard. The 50th? Not so much. But whether you're just starting out, or a cube-making machine, every time you get the finished form in your hands you should pat yourself on the back. Be proud. You earned it!

BASIC SHAPES

GETTING TRICKY

64 Balls

It's time to learn your first bonafide trick. This is the one that's going to wow friends and family. Don't have friends? This is the move that changes all of that. Follow closely.

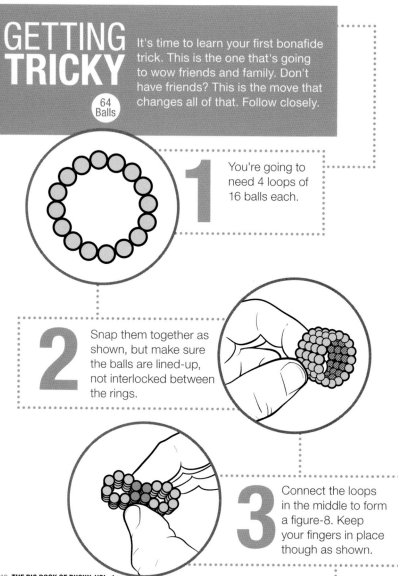

1 You're going to need 4 loops of 16 balls each.

2 Snap them together as shown, but make sure the balls are lined-up, not interlocked between the rings.

3 Connect the loops in the middle to form a figure-8. Keep your fingers in place though as shown.

4 This is it, the moment of truth. We need to add your other hand into this equation though. Put your other thumb and forefinger on the outside of the figure 8. Push inwards as you release your fingers from the middle. Go go go...

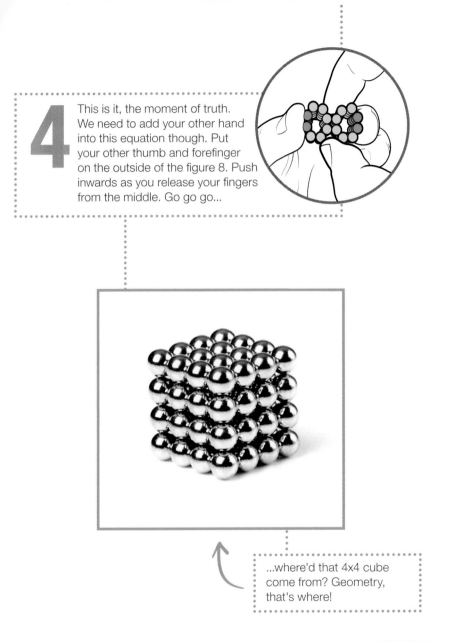

...where'd that 4x4 cube come from? Geometry, that's where!

50 GREATEST BUCK'D-UP MOVIE LINES

It's true, sometimes it's easy to Buck up even your favorite movie lines. Sometimes we do it on purpose... replacing a word with "Bucky" "Balls" or "Buckyballs" just for fun. These are a few of our favorites as suggested by you, the Ballers, in a recent Facebook contest. See if you can guess which movies they come from.

1. Bucky, we have a problem... 2. Those Buckyballs really tied the room together, man. 3. A census taker once tried to test me. I ate his liver with some Buckyballs and a nice Chianti. 4. Say hello to my little Buckyballs. 5. Show me the Buckyballs! 6. Hasta La Vista, Bucky. 7. Patience, my friend. In time, he will seek you out, and when he does, you must bring him before me. He has grown strong. Only together can we turn him to the Bucky Side of the Balls. 8. You want the Bucky? You can't handle the Bucky! 9. These aren't the balls you're looking for.... 10. My name is Bucky balls...you killed my father. Prepare to die. 11. Bucky, I am your balls. 12. Go ahead...Make my Buckyballs. 13. His first night in the joint, Bucky Dufresne cost me two packs of Buckyballs. He never made a sound. 14. Frankly my dear, I don't give a Buckyball. 15. I can't believe I gave my Buckyballs to a geek. 16. They may take our lives, but they'll never take OUR BUCKYBALLS! 17. I love the smell of Bucky in the morning. It smells like...Balls. 18. May the Buckyballs be with you. 19. The greatest trick Bucky ever pulled was convincing the world that he didn't exist. 20. I am Jack's Buckyballs. 21. The first rule of Bucky club is you don't talk about Bucky club. The second rule of Bucky club is you do not talk about Bucky club. 22. Unfortunately, no one can be told what the Buckyball is. You have to see it for yourself. 23. Excuse me, could I have some more Buckyballs? 24. This house is so full of people it makes me sick. When I grow up and get Buckyballs, I'm living alone. 25. You had me at Buckyballs. 26. Excuse me, ma'am—in the leopard dress. You have an amazing set of Buckyballs. 27. Nobody puts Buckyballs

The Amazing Magnetic Desktoy You Can't Put Down!

BUCKY

BUCKY SCHEIDER   BUCKY SHAW   BUCKY DREYFUSS

BUCKY

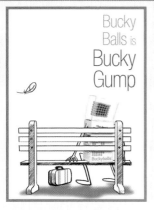

Bucky Balls is **Bucky Gump**

in a corner. **28.** We're not going to leave a baby in the room. There's a f***ing Buckyball in the bathroom. **29.** With enough Buckyballs one could blow up just about anything. **30.** In the past those Buckyballs won't be there, Marty! **31.** All right, Mr. DeMille, I'm ready for my Buckyballs. **32.** Here's lookin' at you, Buckyballs. **33.** When the dog bites. When the bee stings. When I'm feeling sad... I simply remember my Buckyballs, and then I don't feel so bad. **34.** Goodbye mama, now you can have Buckyballs in heaven. **35.** Are you telling me that you men finished your Buckyballs on your own? **36.** To Buckyballs and beyond! **37.** And here's something else, Bob: I have eight different Buckyballs right now. I beg your pardon? Eight Buckyballs? **38.** Get your stinking BALLS off me, you damned dirty ape! **39.** Of all the Buckyball joints in all the towns in all the world, she walks into mine. **40.** I feel the need. The need for Buckyballs! **41.** Maybe there won't be marriage, maybe there won't be sex, but by God there'll be Buckyballs! **42.** I'm here to chew bubblegum and kick Buckyballs...and I'm all out of bubblegum. **43.** Balls? Where we're going, we don't need balls. **44.** It's 106 miles to Chicago, we've got a full tank of Buckyballs, half a pack of cigarettes, it's dark, and we're wearing sunglasses. **45.** As long as people are still having premarital sex with many anonymous partners while at the same time experimenting with mind-expanding Buckyballs in a consequence-free environment, I'll be sound as a pound! **46.** 1...POINT....21...Buckyballs! **47.** Soylent Green is Buckyballs! **48.** Buckyball, I don't know what to say. Lectroids? Planet 10? Nuclear extortion? A girl named John? **49.** No, Sir, I didn't see you playing with your Buckyballs again, Sir! **50.** There are three rules: They don't like light. Don't get them wet. And never, never no matter what feed them Buckyballs after midnight!

FUN FACT

Buckyballs were named for Buckminster Fuller. Who was he? The Internet has all of the answers... but we're happy to share a few. He invented the geodesic dome (a sphere made of triangles—you'll learn how to make it in the pages ahead), coined the term "Space Ship Earth" (referring to the fact that we're all in this together, hurtling through space in a group), and once gave a lecture for 36 straight hours. He was smart. He was crazy. He was fun. Remind you of anything?

BIGGER & BETTER BUCKY

Every journey begins with a single step. You've already taken that first step —it was the basic stuff you just learned. Time to run, jump, and pole-vault Bucky-style! Brace yourself for auto-assembling forms, shapes that bend and twist, and more. Master this section and you'll appear more attractive to the opposite sex, you'll be more likely to get a raise at work, and more likable all around. Or so we'd like to think...

Time to get serious...ish.

BIGGER & BETTER

⓲ THE **HEXAGON**
18 Balls

The Polio vaccine, the downfall of the Berlin wall, the ousting of Paula Abdul from American Idol; some breakthroughs come with great fanfare. Others, not so much. It doesn't mean they're any less important though. Meet the hexagon...

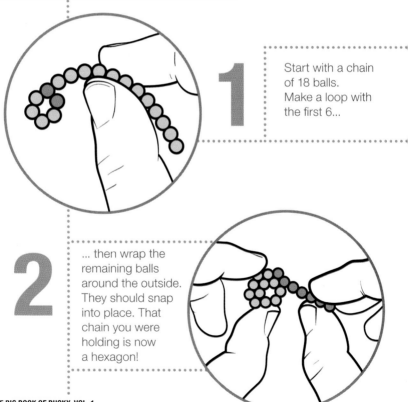

1

Start with a chain of 18 balls. Make a loop with the first 6...

2

... then wrap the remaining balls around the outside. They should snap into place. That chain you were holding is now a hexagon!

FUN FACT

Hexagons are just about the most versatile of all the simple shapes Buckyballs can make. Once you get the balls into this form, they can:

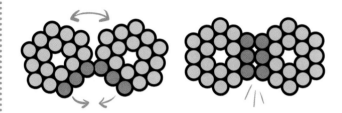

Roll around each other... (Go ahead, take two and turn one around the other. You'll see.)

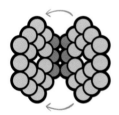

... fold on top of each other, and unfold. All the while holding their shape. Fun, right? Time to put that new found knowledge into action.

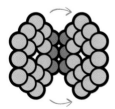

BIGGER & BETTER

Time to build.

Try this... yeah it looks tough, but so did Jean-Claude Van Damme. The truth is, he was just a cheese-ball actor and the tube shown here is just 12 hexagons. All you have to do is snap 'em together. Give it a shot. Nothing hard about it.

216 Balls

Next, take a stab at this snowflake. It's 12 hexagons too. You can see that, right?

216 Balls

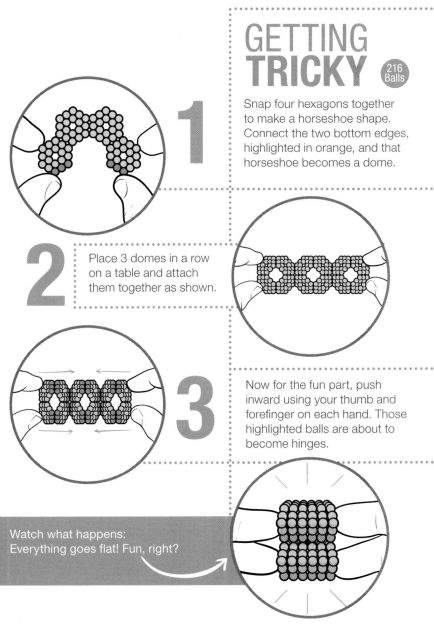

GETTING TRICKY

216 Balls

1 Snap four hexagons together to make a horseshoe shape. Connect the two bottom edges, highlighted in orange, and that horseshoe becomes a dome.

2 Place 3 domes in a row on a table and attach them together as shown.

3 Now for the fun part, push inward using your thumb and forefinger on each hand. Those highlighted balls are about to become hinges.

Watch what happens: Everything goes flat! Fun, right?

THE **BUCKYBALL**

A sphere made of loops made of balls? Don't over think it. It's building time! Ready, steady, go...

This Buckyball is made with 12 loops. There is a bigger version though, shown on the Original Buckyballs packaging. Once you've conquered this beast, see if you can master it's bigger brother.

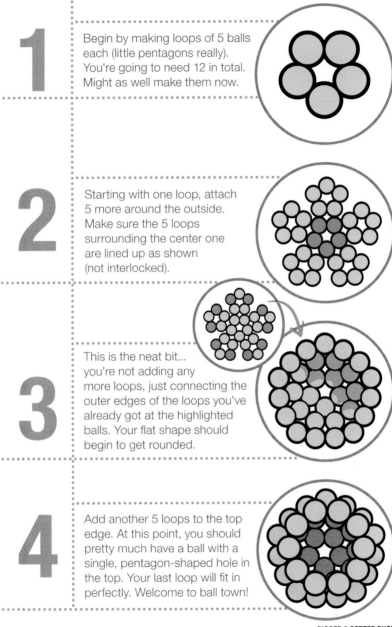

1

Begin by making loops of 5 balls each (little pentagons really). You're going to need 12 in total. Might as well make them now.

2

Starting with one loop, attach 5 more around the outside. Make sure the 5 loops surrounding the center one are lined up as shown (not interlocked).

3

This is the neat bit... you're not adding any more loops, just connecting the outer edges of the loops you've already got at the highlighted balls. Your flat shape should begin to get rounded.

4

Add another 5 loops to the top edge. At this point, you should pretty much have a ball with a single, pentagon-shaped hole in the top. Your last loop will fit in perfectly. Welcome to ball town!

BIGGER & BETTER

TRIANGLES

Ancient Egyptians, the inventor of
Doritos and Arsenio Hall's hairstylist—
Lots of people understand the power
of triangles. Soon you will too...

1

Triangles begin as
a loop of 9 balls.

2

You're just a pinch and a poke
away from perfection. First,
pinch a corner with your
thumb and forefinger
and hold it steady as
you poke the other
side flat with your other
hand. Ultimately, it's the
touching of the highlighted
balls that give it stability.

GETTING TRICKY

Now for the really fun bit. Follow closely, when arranged properly these balls are magic, magic, magic. Unless, of course, you do it wrong. Don't sweat it though, part of the magic is in their ability to forgive.

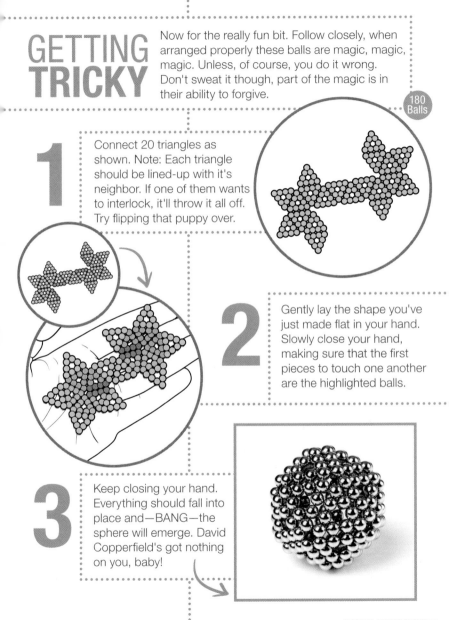

180 Balls

1 Connect 20 triangles as shown. Note: Each triangle should be lined-up with it's neighbor. If one of them wants to interlock, it'll throw it all off. Try flipping that puppy over.

2 Gently lay the shape you've just made flat in your hand. Slowly close your hand, making sure that the first pieces to touch one another are the highlighted balls.

3 Keep closing your hand. Everything should fall into place and—BANG—the sphere will emerge. David Copperfield's got nothing on you, baby!

BIGGER & BETTER

GETTING TRICKY

216 Balls

It takes 24 triangles to make each of the patterns shown. Getting them into position without the wrong bits sticking to one another can be tough, but it's well worth the effort. No really. Once you've gotten either one laid out properly, push on the outside as indicated.

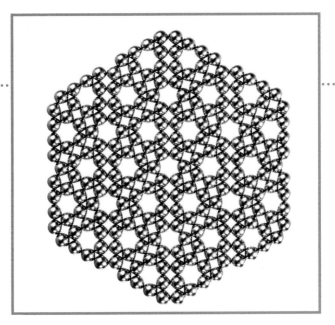

With just a nudge, both patterns become this oversized hexagon made of triangles.
But wait, there's more...

FUN FACT

Buckyballs' magnetic core contains one of 17 "rare earth metals" (they get a special box on the periodic table) called Neodymium. The arrangement of electrons in rare earth elements lets them develop strong magnetic fields. You'll find similar magnets, only larger, in the engines of eco-friendly hybrid cars.

BIGGER & BETTER

Remember that giant hexagon you made of triangles—you should, seriously, it was on the last page—hold onto it. There's still work to be done.

1 Fold the giant hexagon so that the outer edges touch. It should look something like a tube... albeit a fairly intricate one.

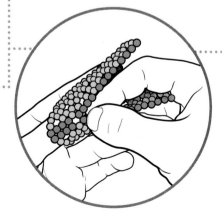

2 Cut open the back edge of the tube. Be delicate though, one wrong move and all is lost.

3
If you did it right, the shape you're left with should look like this... a butterfly.

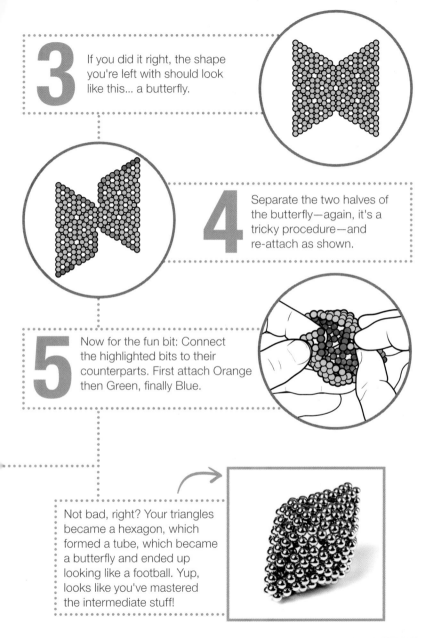

4
Separate the two halves of the butterfly—again, it's a tricky procedure—and re-attach as shown.

5
Now for the fun bit: Connect the highlighted bits to their counterparts. First attach Orange then Green, finally Blue.

Not bad, right? Your triangles became a hexagon, which formed a tube, which became a butterfly and ended up looking like a football. Yup, looks like you've mastered the intermediate stuff!

BUCKY BY THE NUMBERS

"These balls are off the chart!" We've heard it more times than we can count... but it's simply not true. In fact, charting, graphing and otherwise documenting Buckyballs and Bucky-related activities is our second favorite thing to do at work (behind playing with Buckyballs of course). Behold, the fruits of our labor.

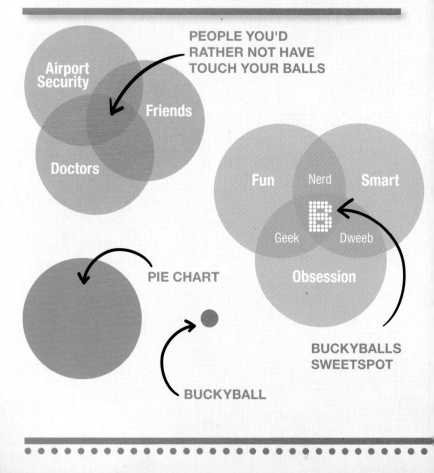

PEOPLE YOU'D RATHER NOT HAVE TOUCH YOUR BALLS

Airport Security

Friends

Doctors

Fun   Nerd   Smart

Geek   Dweeb

Obsession

PIE CHART

BUCKYBALLS SWEETSPOT

BUCKYBALL

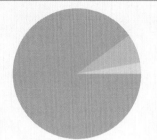

HOW YOU LOST A BUCKYBALL

It ran off with your missing sock

Playing darts on filing cabinet across room

That guy who "Doesn't get it" but "Had to see 'em for himself"

THINGS WORTH WORKING ON AT WORK

Getting a promotion

Balancing the budget

The TPS Report

Documenting your Bucky skills to win a Facebook contest

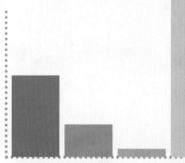

CHANCES OF MESSING UP THE CUBE VS. NUMBER OF PEOPLE WATCHING

Fumble-age

Social Pressure

REASONS TO LEAVE YOUR FRIENDS BEHIND

New Set Of Buckyballs

Your friends don't dance, and if they don't dance, well, they're no friends of mine

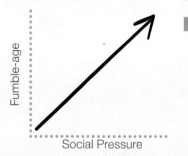

FUN FACT With your help, sales of Buckyballs raised more than $15,000 in 2010 to support the Buckminster Fuller Institute's Buckminster Fuller Challenge, a $100,000 prize awarded to solve humanity's most pressing problems.

BUCKY **ADVANCED**

Playing with Buckyballs isn't rocket science, brain surgery, or quantum physics... but making the shapes contained in this section comes close. Don't be intimidated by the diagrams, take it one step at a time and you'll be making these highly advanced shapes and structures in no time. That, or you'll go insane. Either way, enjoy the ride. The next few pages are like the SAT, MCAT and GMATs combined.

Buckle up for safety.

THE **OCTAHEDRON** (231 Balls)

...That's genius speak for "solid diamond shape." Before you get started, be warned: It takes 231 Buckyballs to complete (more than a single set). Only got one set? Don't worry, we've got 'cha covered. Simply make one of each of the shapes (A, B, C, D) described below and you'll assemble a fairly interesting shape too!

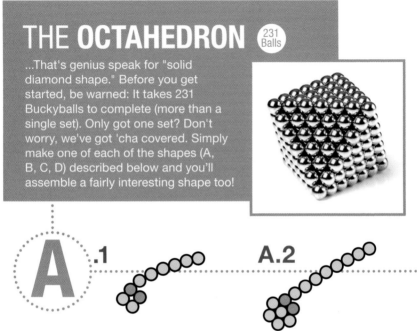

A.1

Start with a chain of 37 balls. Fold the first two balls over forming a square with a very long tail.

A.2

Keep wrapping like you do when making a standard hexagon...

A.3

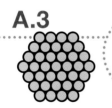

... eventually what you're left with is a hexagon 4 balls wide on each side.

B.1

With a chain of 19 balls, repeat steps A.1 to A.3 to form a hexagon 3 balls wide on each side.

B.2

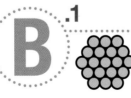

Next, take a chain of 11 balls, and wrap it around 4 sides of the hexagon as shown.

B.3

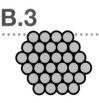

This is the funny shape you're left with. It's unsymmetrical, but we're about to fix that.

B.4

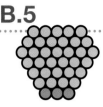

Add a chain of 3 balls to the upper-right side as shown.

B.5

Add a chain of 3 balls to the bottom side as shown. Repeat steps B.1 - B.5 as you'll need two of shape B.

C.1

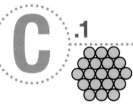

Start with another hexagon 3 balls wide (like the one you made in step B.1).

C.2

Add two balls to both the upper-right and upper-left sides as shown.

C.3

Add a chain of 4 balls to the top.

C.4

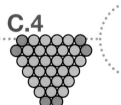

Add two balls to each of the 3 sides. Repeat steps C.1 - C.4 as you'll need two of shape C.

D.1

Again, start with a hexagon 3 balls wide (like the one you made in step B.1).

4.2

Add two balls to each side as shown. Repeat steps D.1 - D.2 as you'll need two of shape D.

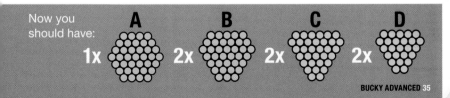

Now you should have:

1x A **2x** B **2x** C **2x** D

BUCKY ADVANCED

5 Now snap them all together as shown. Pay close attention to the diagrams though and notice everything is interlocked, not lined up...

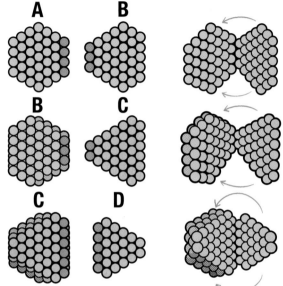

... at this point, if you had enough balls at the start, you've got an extra B, C, and D. Flip the shape in your hand over and repeat step 5.

6 Add 1 ball to each of the 6 corners and you're done!

Still need help? Go to **GetBuckyballs.com/Secret39** to see a video of how it's done.

THE **DODECAHEDRON**

Around BuckyHQ we call this the Whoa-Decahedron. Why? Because not only is it complex as all get-out, it also has the distinction of being one of the few shapes we like making that requires more balls to build than are in the finished product. Really, there are 660 balls in the finished product, but it takes 710 balls (that's several sets of Buckyballs) to build. How do you like them apples?

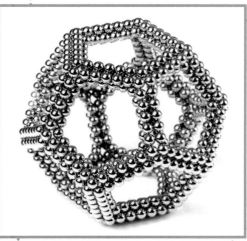

Want more? Go to **GetBuckyballs.com/ Secret40** to unlock a secret video showing how it's done.

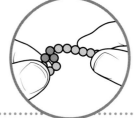

1

Starting with a chain 105 balls long, connect ball 1 to the space between balls 5 and 6 as shown.

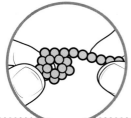

2

Keep wrapping but each additional row of balls should be slightly behind the one before it... the shape you're making is convex, not flat.

3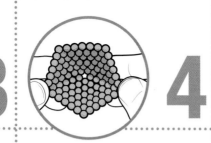

When it's all said and done, you should have a three dimensional pentagon with 7 balls on each side.

4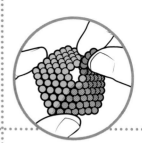

Now for the fun part: Start unraveling from the center. Having trouble? Try attaching a single Buckyball to the center ball and pull.

5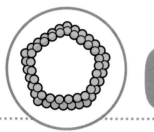

Stop removing balls when you have a pentagon just two rows deep. Note: You're going to need 12 of these in total.

6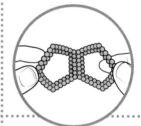

Stick two of these pentagons together. Notice that while the balls in each pentagon are interlocked, the connection between the two is lined up.

7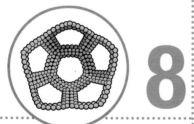

Add 4 more pentagons as shown, so that 5 surround one. Next, take your 6 remaining pentagons and make another of the shape shown.

8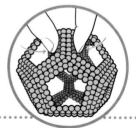

Attach the two halves together to make a whole. Pinch the center rows inward to make it more stable. Be careful though, it's still a delicate beast.

READY? AIM...

GET FIRED. (Please Don't Get Fired)

The best thing about Buckyballs in the office? So much of the
furniture and fixtures are metal... and magnetic. Attach this bullseye to
the nearest filing cabinet, fridge, or co-worker with a plate in his or her
head and practice your Buck'n Chuck'n skills.
Bonus points for cross-cubicle action.

Buckyballs

THE (Extremely Abridged) HISTORY
OF THE DESKTOY

1983: Desperate for something to put on his desk, man turns to science, placing a device known as **Newton's Cradle** between his telephone and pen cup. Minutes later, the thrill of watching balls bang together is lost.

1993: Looking to expel some creative energy, man

places a dish of sand on his desk along with a tiny rake with which to draw lines in it. All happy feelings are lost when the **Zen Garden**'s sand winds up in a keyboard. **1997:** Both creative and fun, the "Pin Art" box feels wonderful to the

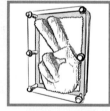

touch... and makes a wondrous place for co-workers and children to leave lewd gestures. **Pin Art** quickly makes its way from the desk, to the home, to the yard sale. **2000-2008:** With the **Internet** no longer just a dream, it seemed physical objects could no longer compete for office-dwellers down-time. 100% of all non work-related attention went to videos of cats doing silly things or stalking exes on Facebook...

2009: Along Came...
Buckyballs

BUCKY
MASTERCLASS

The Bucky creations photographed on the following pages come without instructions, explanations, diagrams, or how-to's. Why? Because this is the Big Book of Bucky Vol. 1, not the Buck'n Library of Congress. No really, they're just that complex. You'll see. You'll also notice that you now know the basic building blocks of just about every shape you're about to see. Let the games begin; the only limits are your imagination.

Be inspired. Dream big. Have fun.

Our Master Shapesmith invented his own
basic building block. Fun, right?

Q*bert. You remember
him right?

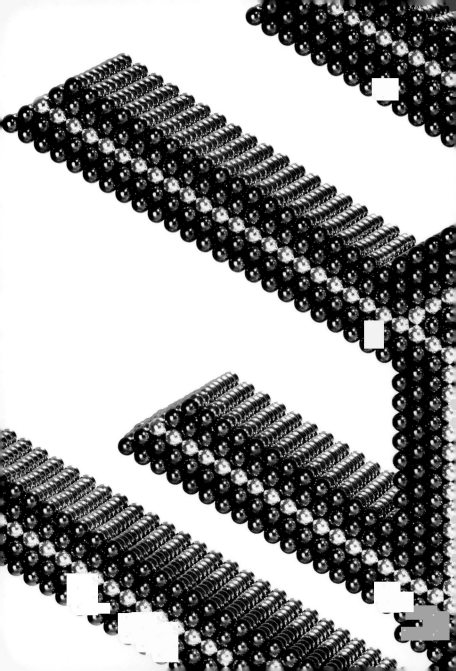

TIE fighters flying
in formation.

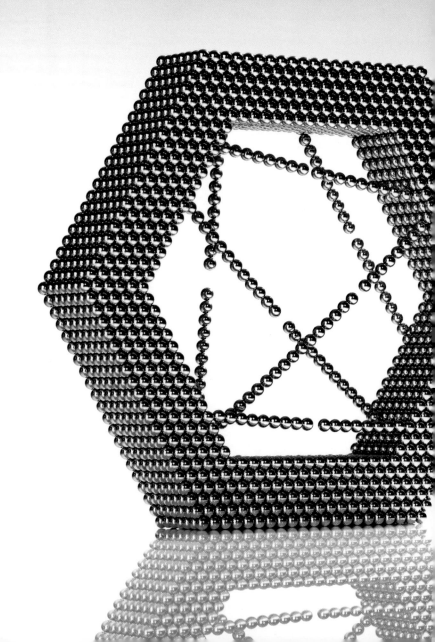

The balls are actually
suspended using magnetism!

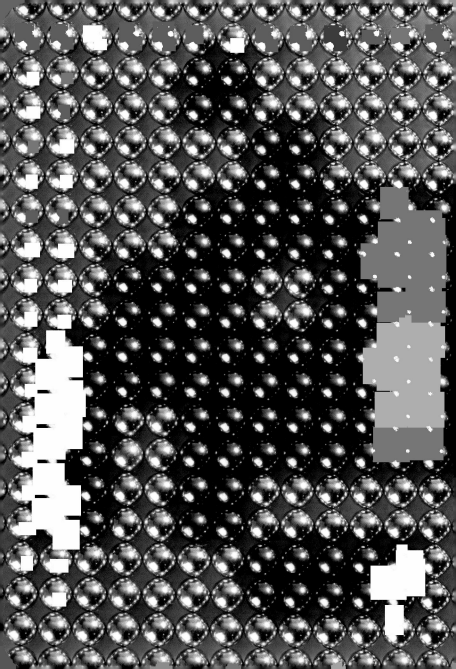

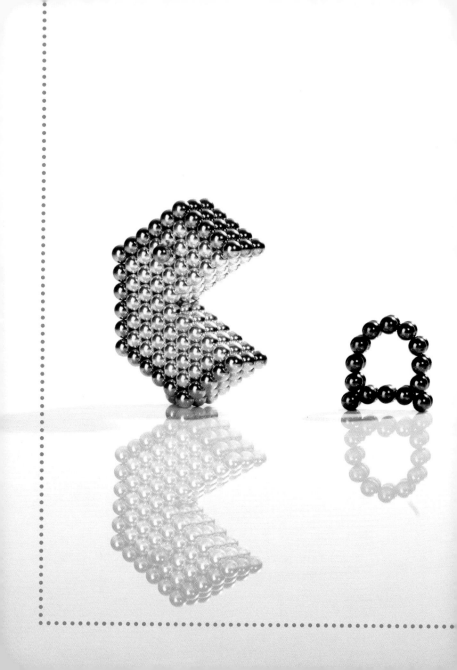

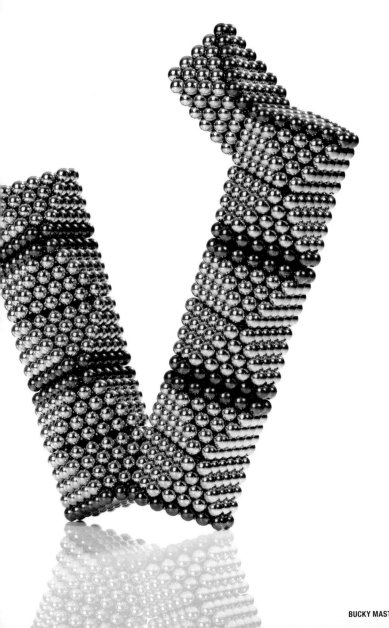

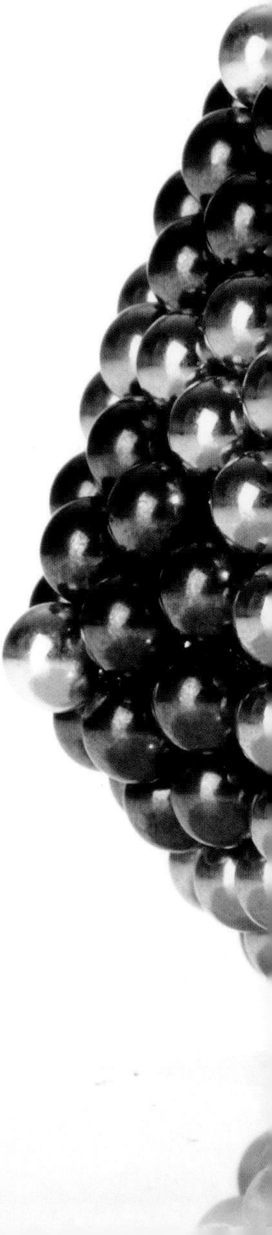

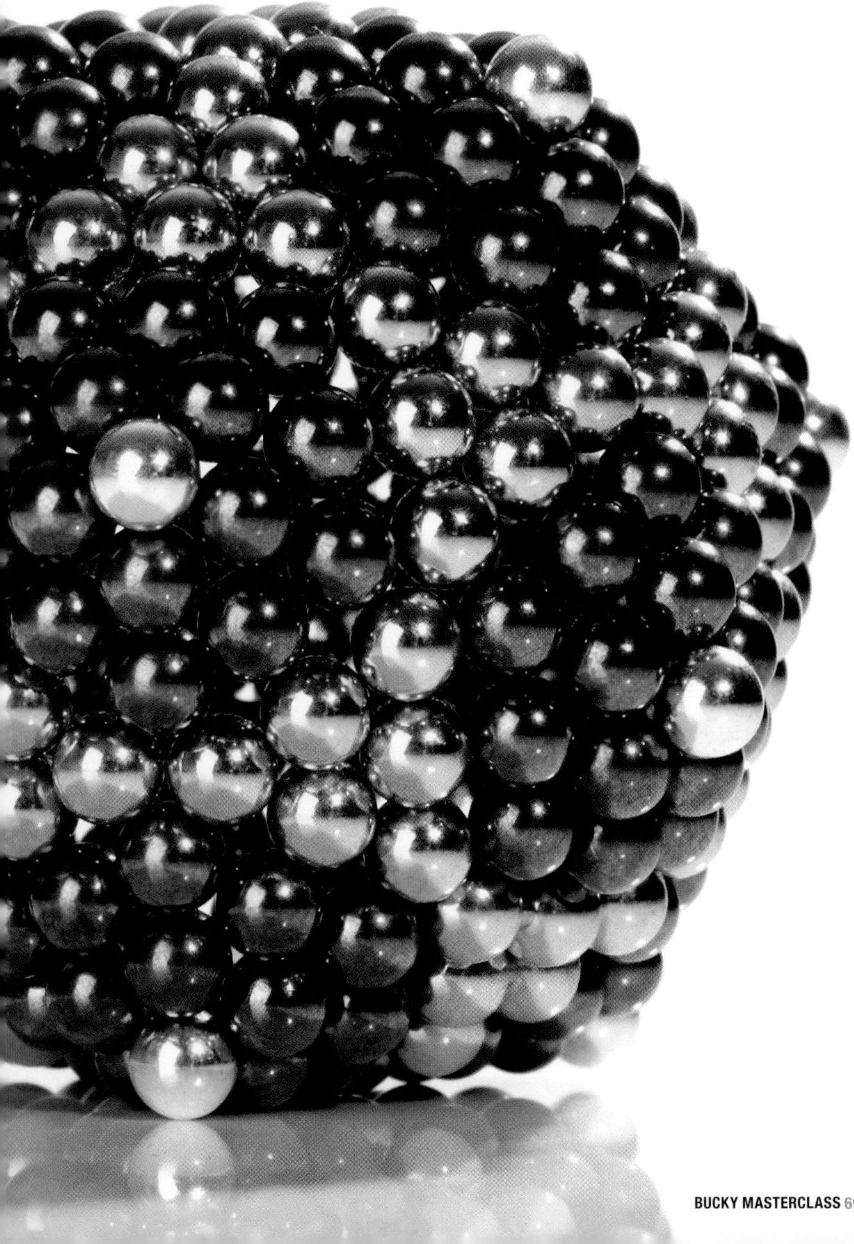

For even more,
check out our blog:
GetBuckyballs.com/blog

BUCKY MASTERCLASS

FROM **OUR FANS**

Sometimes we teach you. Sometimes you teach us. Regardless, all that knowledge is traded daily on our Facebook page. These are a few of our favorite posts from our fans from the past year.

Ranier S.

Josh E.

Judith M.

TIM J. "Geek toys rock. This was made with 824 Buckyballs. I ran out before I could attempt hands or feet though."

Sarah T.

MARIAN W. "I'm always looking for extra pieces to incorporate when I'm building stuff. That ball on top was left in the house when I moved in. It's not magnetic, but the Buckys stuck to it. Not bad, right?"

Yoyo B.

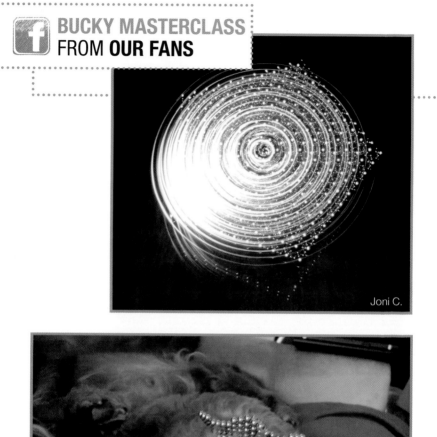

Joni C.

Nick B.

TREY G. "I know Buckyballs and pets don't mix... but this was too cute to avoid and I snatched 'em back off her head before she even knew they were there."

CHECK IT **TWICE**

Before you can claim the diploma on the following page, you'll need to accomplish each one of the tasks listed below. This is just the start though—your MOB (Master of Ballin')—you've still got miles to go. Let your imagination run wild.

UNIVERSITY of Buckyballs

By Decree of the Bucky Board of Ballers
in accordance with the requirements set forth by
the founding Buckys, we hereby confer upon

_____

(your name here)

the Degree

MASTER OF BALLIN'

from the University of Buckyballs.

Maxfield Von Zoom, III

Sir Oberton Doggle